Poetic Melodies in a Minor Key

Blanche Sears

Published by New Generation Publishing in 2020

First Edition

Paperback ISBN: 978-1-80031-810-6
Hardback ISBN: 978-1-80031-809-0

www.newgeneration-publishing.com

New Generation Publishing

Dedication

To Tom, without whom this work would not have come to fruition; to my children, Rachel, Nicholas and Rebecca for unstinting love and support; to my grandchildren for being themselves.

Acknowledgements

With special thanks to friends from the Writing Group – Shirley Hughes, Brigitta Ansdell – Evans, Kerry Beckett, Ted Aves, Robert Lentell and Henry Tegner.
To Alison Carter for helpful advice about publishing.
To Ruth O'Callaghan for useful discussion and permission to publish 'Germination' from 'Cold Weather Shelter Anthology 2020.'

Contents

WRITING

Writing Group

I gather words and throw them into the air,
Hoping they'll descend in an inspired order.
Then dip into my bag of commas, capitals, full stops
And arrange them on the page to be deciphered.

The silken purse of ideas is almost empty,
But my searching fingers pry into the corners,
Smooth the pleats, press the lines straight,
And find a few gems of inspiration.

The interpreter will be you; roused from your musings,
Your task to weave my patterns into sense,
Yet leaving some secrets for others to discover.
To my emotions you each contribute your own,
Sort through the pile, identify, share, reject,
Slot into spaces, places, time-warped reminiscences.

The exercise complete, you each take away a version
That is yours alone, a personal translation.

As for myself, I re-read, tear up and start again.

Germination

Ideas flourish like seeds planted in receptive soil.
They lie dormant, watered from time to time
By tears of joy, sadness, frustration, release.
The warmth of human contact acts like spring rain.

Beguiled by labels of 'Lathyrus Oderatus',
'Labra Dorica Purpurea' and 'Clematis Flammula',
I scatter my seeds like Van Gogh's semeur,
Or Ophelia in her madness.

The touch of life I leave to God or nature.

There's fennel for fasting; rosemary for remembrance;
Salvia for sagacity; chives and chicory.
Spikenard from the Bible; perfumed roses from Isfahan;
Dandelions to test your French; deadly hemlock for
Anglo-Saxon.

'Cover me lightly,' the packet states, 'or not at all.'
'Exercise patience for results. One will be rewarded
With swards of green and mauve and pink,
A feast for the eye and buds for taste.'

Soon there will be music in the soughing of the leaves
And a touch of poetry in the sweetness.

The Searching

I have discovered a god within myself,
My own Higgs boson particle.
It talks. I listen. Question authority
When necessary. Obey blindingly
On occasions. Doubt frequently, 'I
Am the Resurrection and the Life.'
Feel Immortality in memories of
Others, in recalled words and actions.
I have taken Ishmael's cry and Hagar's
Rejection as my own; agonised with
'It is finished' from the cross;
Placed stones on neglected tombs to
Wake the dead into remembrances;
Sought enlightenment in bells and monosounds;
Rejected food to sharpen inward resolution;
Sailed with Woden to Valhalla and
Played Leda to Zeus' swan;
Tasted Heaven in my lover's arms
And Hell in children's sufferings,
Immediate and through war.

Play me a Schubert impromptu, my god,
A melody of Mozart, deep chords of Beethoven,
Songs without words, and my discovery
Will be complete, confirmed.

Poetry

The beat of the rhythm,
The pulse of the line,
Inspiration in a phrase,
A name – Achilles, Antigone,
Macbeth, Lear, Henry V.
A web woven for mortals,
To inspire fear,
Love, admiration, the
Desire to achieve.

All language leads to Heaven and Hell.
The power of the universe lies in words.
They are the ropes that bind us together.
Taut strings to the past, whips to ambition,
Curbs to folly.

Words clothe the magic of thought,
Conveying through stories the strength of
Connection, remonstration, warning, exultation.
More powerful than the sword.
More lasting.

Stories

Stories are the poetry of speech,
Expressing emotion, ambition, rejection,
Confession, aspiration, betrayal.
A vehicle for gladness, sadness, mystery, History.

Gather round the table with King Arthur.
Blow the horn with Roland at Ronçesvalles.
Charge for your country behind Henry V.
Weep for the Babes in the Wood or be
Beguiled for a Thousand and One Nights.

Ease Death through visions of the Elysian Fields,
Valhalla, Enlightenment, Heaven.
Create your own dreamland with the words
'Once upon a time.'

Reflections

The river glides over the stones,
Carrying away small pebbles like ideas
Swept into the main stream
Or hidden forever in the sandy bank.

Look closer.

Relics of lives float by - papers, cotton,
A child's plastic toy, a single glove,
A broken brooch, a coin or two.
Hidden lives to be explored.

Seize the ideas; give me a pen
Before they disappear, or release me now
And let me go with the flow, shedding
My thoughts, abandoning words that fall
Untranslated on to the page.

Each moment passes, catches the sunlight
Then is gone forever.

Snow Speak

The snow sets the silence talking,
Each flake an artistry of expression,
Shifting and drifting in syllables,
Punctuated by flurries and snowstops.

Words pile up, covering the uneven ground of dialogue,
Blending into the one-ness and universality of lives.
The silence of birds is replaced by children's cries of joy
As they toboggan down slopes unrecognizable from
contours.

Freed from the tyranny of car and train and plane
We learn to take our steps once more; discover language;
Exchange phrased pleasantries, paragraphed on glacial
surfaces;
Retreat to homes comma-ed off by an enforced freedom.

The semi-colon of disruption passed, through drops of
thaw
We brace ourselves to tackle chapters of familiarity,
Yet haunted still by icicles that stirred
Strange longings in short stories of another world.

WAR

Sacred Earth

This soil looks the same as at home,
Dark, crumbling, pebbled.
Yet it is different.
Here the pebbles are my diamonds,
Hewn on the battlefield and splashed with your blood.

I finger them, as yet unpolished, and wipe away the dirt,
Making them shine, as you would have done, my son,
Had time and Fate allowed.

I catch no gleam from your medals. My poppy does not glow.
The dull red sheds no light upon my gloom.
But I will lay it on your grave
For honour and in everlasting remembrance.

Counselling Session

'Bare your soul,' they said.

I took a poppy and crushed it in my palm.
The red juice filled the crevice of my lifeline
Like hot blood flowing,
Scenting with bitterness the unresponsive hand.

'Bare your heart,' they said.

I took your letters tied with ribbon,
Their paper thin like tissue tearing,
Your medals and your ring, and laid them on the wood.
The gold reflected cold against the grain.

'Bare your pain,' they said.

I squeezed out last drops of sadness that hung
Behind tired eyes, all pleasure gone.
Recalled remembered words and lived again the
Time I saw you last.

I have bared all; but the baring has not
Eased the burden. The poppy has not brought sleep.
Remembering has not brought release.
Consoling words hang emptily in space.

They cannot teach me how to bear.

‘Share your pride,’ they said.

I took the letters, the medals, and the ring,
A bold circumference of memories encompassing
A lifetime’s passion, and proudly gave them to the world.

Known Only Unto God.

Without a name we are nothing.
Unidentifiable. Nonentities.
As with places, names give us
Their history, their time-set at a glance.

Take Dulwich, the settlement where the dill grew.
Chester, a camp from Roman times.
Abergavenny, commanding the mouth of a river.
Shields, the fishermen's huts on the foreshore.
York and Thwaite, recalling Viking hordes.

Choose names carefully, young parents, in case your offspring
Are embarrassed by your choice; but don't be pressurised
By another's will. Children can change'Archibald' for 'Cary'
'Shane' or 'Wayne'. Select 'Obadiah' if you wish
To join 'Apple', 'Gaga',' 'Ivy', 'Snowdrop'.
It's your right. Wear your 'Poppy' with pride.

Only if you are the Unknown Soldier will you be
Covered in glory, heralded, honoured.
To millions of mothers whose sons lie somewhere, or nowhere,
Does the unknown give everlasting assurance of recognition.

Sacrifice.

I asked for roses, sweetly perfumed.
You gave me poppies, opium-washed.
I asked for life. You gave it fleetingly
But generously, a sublimation and a joy.
I asked for love; but then you left
To serve another life, another love,
To which you gave your all.
You willed me memories, but also pain so deep
That remembering is a constant sorrow.
  How then shall I respond if our son says,
"I want to be a soldier like my Dad,"
Demanding as it may my sacrifice
A second time?

PLACES

The Pier at South Shields

Into my life there stretches still the pier.
Always, like a probing finger of stone,
It reaches through the sea fret of battered years.
I feel once more the coldness of the rocks, the fascination
Of the lighthouse with its beam that comes and goes,
Challenging the waves that lap the lichens lovelessly.
The storm gates open. The light beckons.
A child again, I go to find the tiny china dolly
Nestling in the structure of the solid lighthouse wall,
A careless symbol stuck with aimless jest into
The hardening concrete aeons ago. Generations
Have passed this way to touch with superstitious hope
The umbilical embryo of human life. Below
The waves ignore our thoughts, obliterate in
One swelling motion the wholeness of existence,
Backwards and forwards, tossing through the wrack
Of ending days our futile hopes and memories.
The foghorn moans. Caught by the mist
I turn towards the sand and through the stretching
Of the years take my steps unerringly, unfalteringly
Into the water, to live again the enchantment of childhood.

Northern Lights

I tear you from my memory like
An old newspaper cutting – day, date, year,
Aeons ago when we romped the mounds of
Sand that overlooked the sea; licked
Sugared cream frozen in years, now melting
With recollections of what was,
What might have been.

Above us the Souter lighthouse, first to shine,
Challenging the waves that beat the shore.
Along the coast still stood the Marsden rock,
A Fingal's cave of the North, its arch
Recalling an old church, its slippery stones enticing.
There we prised limpets from the rocks and
Mussels in binding ropes, with flakes of orange
Glimpsed through broken shells.

Gone is the grotto now, claimed by the
Triumphant sea. As the light fades catch
The sad sighs of lost sailors, echoing
Through the darkness. Moan again foghorn.
Souter, flash your beam across the advancing tide.

On Visiting Berkeley Castle

Time has tamed their greatness.
Where once proud Mortimer revelled
Now grow the daisy, speedwell, buttercup.
I pick a flower to press in memory
But it fades in moments and the petals fall.

Beguiling, treacherous Isabella fled home
To France. Here among the ruins sheep
Have their eyes pecked out by crows,
Imitating the death throes of her King
In Berkeley Castle. Red hot pokers
Flourish in country gardens, the irony unnoticed.

What beauty is there now in history?
Let me emerge into the light of the real.
Bombs in Syria. Cries of dying children
Choking on poisonous gas. Christians,
Muslims, Jews killing each other in the name of
Their one God, and praying for victory.

Wake me when the noise has stopped.

A Leper's Spirit Revisits St.Nicholas's Church, Harbledown, Canterbury

I remember the first sign. The thickening spot,
Growing imperceptibly and insidiously until the rot
Set in. I recall in eyes of friends the look
Which spoke of alienation. Finally they took
Me ailing, to the Lepers' Church and left me there.

It's hard to be alone, afraid. The little time I'd got
Lengthened through each dull second until the hot
Affliction parted flesh from flesh and bone from bone.
I prayed to God, crouched on floor of stone,
While men gave silver pennies washed with care.

I begged for alms, shielded distorted limbs from eyes
That spoke their condemnation. 'God's wrath!' their lies
Proclaimed. 'A curse!' Yet Kings have suffered too,
But riches and their power kept all from view.
With body wracked by pain, I lingered in despair.

Then Christ showed mercy, comforted me at length,
When illness and disease sapped all remaining strength.
My soul then left this place, and the contagion passed.
Erroneously I had believed I was the last
To suffer. But now another plague hangs in the air.

Though mankind calls it by another name

It seems to suffering eyes it's much the same.
I see the weakened limbs, all quality of life
Destroyed. Lover from lover, child from mother,
Wife from husband torn. Yet still

High on a windy hill, the church commands its space.
Lacking the prominent columns of Thomas à Becket's
place
Though solid in construction, on Saxon Herebeald's Dun
It offers everlasting peace to all who come.

Somerset Levels, 2014

Soft murmurings of waves disguise
The horrors to come.
Find me the Ark of Ararat
Lord, to prepare for the worst.

Lulled by gentle lappings
We ignore the warning signs
And expect mild Spring tides only.

Now come the winds striking and smiting,
Surpassing even Poseidon in his anger,
Destroying crops, homes, cattle, lives.

Turner would have understood. Never one
To underestimate the power of the sea,
The drownings, the drowned, each brush stroke
Destructive in its advancing tide.

Hospital Ward

I opened a gate in the maze of my mind and found you there,
Locked away, a perfect entity, co-existing with the mainstream
Of my life and yet apart.Six beds waiting, re-assuring.
The well, forgetting soon, think not of you. The dying,
Already gone ahead, no longer are aware.
Only, we the temporarily ill, nestling in the closeness of your care,
Trust ourselves to strangers more than friends,
Surrender to the tyranny of clock and pulse and waves,
Take opiates to dull the pain, obliterate the self.
Accept unquestionably the plasma, pills, bold exercise routines;
Become inured to vomit, blood and smells.
Six bodies in each cell we stick together to instil a feeling of
Endurance, care, respect, from one to all.
We love the young who hover selflessly round margins of our pain
And praise the surgeons for their skill with knife and cutting saw.
Mended, we break away, depart with fond farewells and gestures intimate.
Gently, I ease you back and silently remembering, close the gate.

Seaduction

My feet leave an impression in the wet sand.
I move my toes to stamp it into permanence-
My mark on the world. The waves return,
Curl round the outline, insinuate into spaces,
Bubble round ankles with persuasive touches,
Wanting to converse, to enjoy.

Why have you taken so many? I ask.
Are you never satisfied that you must
Draw another into your arms with
Soft kisses, sweet splashes, pretended exchanges,
Cajoling with whispered sprays and caresses?

In your depths the mariners' bones lie bleached.
Carcasses of ships are motionless, all passion passed.
Seaweed strangles the brave who dared
Your wars, your storms, your enticements.
You have taken the cliffs and dwellings,
Smashed the rocks to fragments to satisfy your lust.

You grave of grandfathers, fathers, friends,
You will not possess me yet.
I retreat from your power into soft sand,
Pick up the ball and play the game of life again

To Tom

In the evening of my life
As the tide runs out apace
Let me stand upon the steep cliff top
Where the sea and sky embrace,
And the mackerel and the spume entwine,
Where gargantuan billows roar,
Remembering how I loved you then
And love you now the more.

The tide is out and now the sea
Laps at the sand's rough edge.
A miracle of poetry in shimmering pools
In trembling wind-ruffled syllables
In moss-fringed hinterland spiked with shells,
I saw it there carved on damp sand
Rough- edged with beats of metric force,
The sea had washed and left.

Too soon, the echoes came
From hollow stones and murmuring caves
Delivered with tremulation by the midwife wind.
Stillborn and silent, cold and far away
The poem and the story within the sand they lay.

MODERN LIFE

Who needs TV. when you've got a tree?

I said 'Good Morning' to my tree.
Its leaves rustled and I knew it understood.
It is the first thing I look at after 'Breakfast'
And the last thing at night to check the 'Weather
Forecast.'
From morning to evening shadows it is my 'Gardeners'
World',
Giving subtle hints of growth to the uninitiated.
It has the 'X Factor', surviving elimination;
Competes with 'Strictly Come Dancing' in the curves
And movement of its branches in the wind.
The birds indulge it with parrot chatter, eluding
Commentaries from 'Nature's Quest.'
The squirrels, never red, escape to their hidden dreys
Without the threat of a predatory 'Master Chef',
Dreaming of constructing towers of inedible exoticism.

On summer days I sit under a canopy of shade
In my black garden chair, knowing that my friend,
Having lived through centuries, will furnish me
With all the answers to 'Mastermind.'
As my feet scrabble the soil at its roots
It whispers tantalising promises that a three day dig
May uncover vast hoards of treasure
To sublimate the discoveries of 'Time Team.'

I touch the tree's gnarled bark; let my fingers linger
In the wrinkles of the bole, knowing it has no need of
being
'Ten Years Younger'- or a hundred come to that.
It will endure unless a showman from 'Grand Designs'
Tears up the corner of my plot in his 'Escape to the
Country'.
But when it is 'The Final Score'
And the 'Weakest Link' consigns its trunk to
conflagration,
Be sure as sparks fly in the great 'Apocalypse'
A voice from above will sound triumphantly,
'You're Fired!'

Negative Equity.

White leaves, lacking the depth of Autumn's colour,
Flutter persistently yet hopefully into our lives,
Pale relics of another's cast-off dreams. Rife
With ring mains and panes of double glass,
All bathrooms fully-tiled, deep freezes packed,
Homes pass in euphemistic phrases to beguile the soul.
Patios, verandahs, houses of character requiring
Modernisation, gentrification, sterilisation,
They pluck the pennies from unwary hands.
Deposits paid, contracts exchanged, bank loans secured,
We join the many millions mortgaged-racked,
Heedless as Faust. The Mephistophelian agent smiles,
Pockets his fee; while we, vacantly possessed,
Shut fast our doors on life. And in the shadows patiently
The Debt Collector waits.

Natural Instincts

With jutting beak, head momentarily poised,
Lurching backwards and forwards with a pincer
movement,
The crow pecks out the life of a squirming worm.
Then moves along the park way, the old manor way,
Though the manor and its nobility have long gone.

Other crows savage rubbish bins, extract scraps of food,
Crisps, apple cores, sandwich fillings, meat, fish, egg,
Scatter the orange bags of Sainsbury's, the green and
white
Of Waitrose, the yellow, blue and red of Lidl
So declaring their patronage universal.
With satisfied caws they sharpen claws, once more
To tear their gains, driven by instinct,
Ignoring our condemnation.

In comfortable armchairs we scan the newspapers,
Ignore the cries of the starving, the dying, those
Voting or fighting for liberty. Mildly condemn or
Appear even sympathetic to people caught out in scams,
Exaggerated expenses claims, inflated bonuses.
Then after a hard day's work, we pour a glass or two of
wine
And tuck into a juicy steak for supper.

Soundless

Your world is full of sounds
While mine is silent.
You touch the piano keys
And play me Beethoven,
Not appreciating the irony.

I have not endured the bellow of guns
In Afghanistan, the explosions in Syria,
The blast of bombs in Boston.
Yet my world is not golden.

I envy you your silver one.
I know speech only from movements of lips,
Smiles of friends, expressions on faces,
Pressure on hands.

I have learnt to interpret your words.
Attempt my own communication,
Exchange gestures.
But all remains quiet.

Do not complain of noise-
Cars hooting, sirens screeching, music blaring.
You have the sound of laughter, a child's first word,
The song of the nightingale, the note of the skylark.

I did not hear you when you said goodbye.

Remember Ozymandias *

Who gives most? Those with millions, billions.
Who scheme and count in gold like Silas Marner,
Realizing perhaps too late that golden hair
Is more valuable than bright metal?
Those who founded churches or cathedrals, built
To save their souls from the torments of hell?
Or the father who after the Great War gave his last £100
saying,
'You have taken my four sons, now take the rest.'
Do we feel good about putting our spare change into a
Salvation Army box, then going home and opening a
bottle of Chablis
To cheer us up?
Better perhaps to give spontaneous help when flood water
threatens.
Or spending moments with a stranger anxious to
unburden,
Never to know the full impact of our conversation.
Words spoken to the man on the bridge contemplating
suicide.
Time spent with family and friends – a stock market
Of perpetual interest, where the widow's mite gains daily.

Remember Ozymandias.

- Shelley's poem

Four Digits, Please

Why are we no longer free? Lost identity.
'Postcode, please. Forgotten? Think of a Password.'
'Rm. 101?' I suggest facetiously.
No smile cracks the ageless face. Botox
Has done its best, made its profit.

'Date of birth,' demands the building society clerk.
I push my piece of paper under the screen
That discourages communication with my fellow men.
Loudly she repeats my answer to the waiting queue,
Intimate details shared with all.
In the supermarket I buy bread, cheese and wine,
And at the checkout hear, 'Enter your number now.'
'6789.'

Desperate to recapture my individuality I seek the open road
And head for Amersham, like Adelstrop, a memorable name,
To find a violet by a mossy stone, pausing only
To pay the congestion charge. 'Tap in four digits, please.'
'1984.'
Does no one merit recognition anymore?
No strife, just freedom-passed through life.

Another World

You have stolen away into silence, my child,
Conversation irrelevant, all eye contact lost.
Escaped into a world where virtual becomes reality.
You hold your existence in the palm of the hand.
Gestures have replaced words as your finger moves
Mechanically over the glass in a small black pad.

Once I believed in Myths, the Tooth Fairy, Father
Christmas.
Felt the weight of knowledge through restless turning of
pages.
Tasted Autumn in blackberries ripened by the sun.
I long to share your thoughts, but the gap is too great.
Wifis, Apps and Kindles - alien concepts all.

You did not say goodbye, but quietly withdrew
Into other imaginings. I shall leave silently
To return to my world.

Bring Back Maths?

2/3 plus 3/4
Make what?
Where is my primary maths,
The joy of figures,
Squiggles and appendages?
I liked the squares,
The little '2s' and '3s'
Cubes and tubes but
Reduced to fractions and
Percentages ---no!
Life's just too short.

Teachers

What we have achieved lingers somewhere in the minds
of children.
Learning, they accept; forget quickly; leave and grow.
Only in the silences of maturity, in remembered pauses,
In recollecting with their children, do we survive.
Their thanks are whispered through the years long after
Our dust lies scattered over terms of succeeding
generations.

Gwyneth Called.

Gwyneth called and left me flowers,
Dahlias - exquisitely formed petals,
Closed, curled like shells clustered on rocks,
Or pointed and bi-coloured.
With pinks as fierce as sunlight.
And yellows to rival Van Gogh's,
Deep wine-velvet, dark with hidden secrets.
Kindness in a vase, given freely.

As the sun falls and darkness encroaches,
My dahlias become nightlias, scentless beauties
Made scented by attar of friendship.

Tomorrow I shall take out my paints.

On Receiving a Redundancy Notice

O deleted, dejected, doubly dundant,
Dolorous, despondent!
Whither the way now ?
Limitless days of atrophied leisure,
Severance tears, watering the growth
Of hidden seedlings. New challenges.
Old friendships renewed. Farewells.
Sweetened days of sunshine and
Time……time……time.

Mary, Queen of Scots

I bought your life for 50p.
Charity shop. Remaindered.
In print you will live forever,
Misunderstood, miscalculating, mismatched.
I've laughed with you through the French years,
Known François and Marie of Guise, brought to life
From the dark pages of history. You
Dance again with Darnley, deliver James,
Bargain and lose with Boswell.
You who ruled realms and men, left friendless, headless,
A little dog alone to mourn your passing.
Sic transit gloria mundi.

PERSONAL

Hidden

In the curl
    of the lip
        of the womb
            it slept, your child.
The baby that was hiding from you,
Its foetal breaths like whispers, imagined infant sighs.

It turned,
    unfurled a little,
        and for an instant,
            Gazed.

Then slipped
    over the rim
        of the cup of its world,
            to twist and swirl

Hiding everlastingly in the maze of time,
Leaving a tear on the cheek and a tear in the heart.

Adoption

The coverlet edge is kissed with sleep.
In feather-light, goosedown lightness
Masking innumerable flutters of anxiety,
The child dreams.
I, who parent am by choice, not nature, divine
The myriad cells to which I have no access,
And think of you the mother tied by blood,
Who protesting, rejecting, departing gave
Solomon that moment to decide.
Love petals, piled high like pillows,
Protect us all against ourselves and blunt
The edge of the sword at our hearts.

A Bird in his Throat

Our son has a bird in his throat. He was born that way.
Deep in the box of his neck an egg was laid.
Nurtured by milk and warmth and love it cracked.
And the bird began to grow, softly feathered, its
Exploratory trills and semi-tones,
Half escaping from an imagined world,
Where lyres and shawms, harps and flutes recalled
A Pan-like idyll. With age the bird began to sing.
Full-throated melodies extinguishing plaintive longings,
Engaging with trumpets and cymbals and drums.
We were proud of our son and loved his singing bird.
But birds and sons grow up and fly the nest.
The singing bird has gone. The branch is bare.
We are left remembering in sadness, awaiting another
Spring.

University Library, 3am.

Books scatter words like crumbs before the wind,
And I, poor sparrow, fly to catch the dainties
Before the carrion crows of literature swoop and snatch
Your offerings, guard them in the recesses of shelves,
To gorge in private.

Only a glint of light, a splash of blue on vellum,
Marks me here in semi-darkness,
Searching out your knowledge,
And digesting.

The library creaks like an old man.
Feathered owls perch silently on the spines,
Guarding their hoards.

With a flash of motivation, in the blink of an eye,
I snatch your provender, to survive,
And grow in wisdom.

Inheritance

I will not leave you gold and silver
Or diamonds, cold with the glint of death,
Reflected in the wrenchings of the spade;
Emeralds, green with the envy of the lesser rich;
Rubies, red with the blood of miners' hands;
Black jet, like shards of forgotten memories
That pierce the indulgent flesh.

Instead I drop small gems of wisdom
Into your opening shells, sands of kindness,
Loyalty, friendship, words of encouragement
Like virtues, bigger than a banker's bonus,
And interest that accumulates through life.
Grow my cultured pearls, lapped by the waves of
Time. Remember, children, you are my jewels.

The Web

A Poem for Adults and perhaps Children.

Three children sat upon the bed
When eagerly the youngest said,
"Now Grandma, will you kindly, please,
Teach us to knit? We have the wool.
It will be fun like going to school."

Grandma agreed. The game began.
While needles clicked the children sang
In unison, 'In, over, off, in, over, off.'
Great times were had, no chance to scoff.
With fingers deft the loops did fly
Like birds ascending to the sky.
Purl followed plain, again and again.

The scarves grew long with colours gay
To drive the winter's cold away
When instantly, the three transformed
To adults upon life's journey stormed.
Till fate or Fates did intervene.
Clotho, Lachesis, Atropos seen
To spin, to weave or knit, to cut,
And suddenly upon the floor
Three intricately - patterned lives –
No Four!

Anniversary

You are the love I dreamed of,
And the dream came true.
No one so loyal, devoted,
In sadness, in happiness.
Helpful, understanding, inspirational.
My dearest beloved,
My Tom.

To Tom on our Wedding Anniversary

In giving me love you gave me life,
Science and Literature united.
Intertwined the joys increased,
With children beautiful to complete our tryst.

We have striven to make our union perfect,
Discovered together the simple things to
Make them great.
Always we have shared our sorrows
And dared the unknown, trusting that
Our mutual love would protect us.
Happy Universary, my darling

WORLD EVENTS

Last Boarding for Düsseldorf - March 2015

The mountains have enclosed you now.
Gathered your souls from the debris of life.
Breathed sustaining air into your torn bodies.
Tears of families momentarily melt
The snow on the icy slopes, before a chill
Encases the past and denies the future.

I strain to catch your last words through the
Creak of icicles. The rush of the wind
Accentuates your plane's descent.
I can never share your parting thoughts,
The final comforts of friends or strangers,
Their hopes extinguished and their lives cut short.

For many left behind there can be no healing,
With pain so deep, with agony inconsolable.
Only Nature can compensate for what man destroyed.
In the cradle of her encompassing mountains
She cherishes their immortality.

Skiing to Heaven

(Belgian Coach Crash 2012)

The slopes gleam white tonight.
Frost glistens; the mountain top stands proud.
I see the ridges made by your skis where
You played and laughed.
Sadness dulls my brain but again
I hear your shouts of joy as you
Race over the summit, down the hill
To be the first, to be the last.

In my pocket wrapped in its envelope
Like a shroud, is your letter.
It arrived today to say,
'Having a wonderful time. See you soon.'

A cold moon shines over the tunnel
Where runnels of water are turned into ice.
You diced with death.
Death won.

Revelation

Each year on the same date, at the same time,
The old man lit his candles to remember
Those he had lost.
Like ghosts they floated before him.
No tears filled his eyes. His grief was too deep.

Then he remembered, word for word,
His boyish questioning of the Rabbi
On that day to change all days.

* * *

'How do I know God exists?' he asked.
'My son,' the Rabbi replied, pondering his Talmud,
'God is everywhere.
In the face of your wife Rebecca,
In the smile of your son Isaac,
In the candles of your Sabbath Seder.'

'Yes,' he said, 'but how do I know?
Give me some proof.'
'Open your holy book,' instructed the Rabbi,
'And read what Jehovah said to Joshua
When he asked for a sign.'

The boy opened and read,

‘When the wind stirs the tops of the mulberry trees,
God is there.’
He looked out of the window.

It was 11.15 am on September 3rd 1939
As the Nazis marched into Berlin.
He saw the wind moving the leaves of the trees
In the Unter Den Linden, near the Karl Marx Strasse,
Near the Brandenberg Gate.

And he knew.

FRIENDS

To Odette *

I stepped through the stars to see you again
And the dust sprinkled and sparkled on my feet.
You approached smiling, extended your hand,
Clasped mine in a familiar gesture,
Then persuasively drew me into your cloud.

We talked about the old days and the young days,
Shared moments of heightened pleasure, sadness,
Success, friendship, fun; dreamtimes
To sustain us in the bad times.

I miss you now.

* A star has been named in her memory

To Jane

You tip-tapped your way into my life
Along paths, corridors and stairs.
Standing silently in the lift you
Gave a deft touch to button number 5.
The light may have gone from your eyes
But is balanced by the laughter in your voice.

You shared your life with me on that level only,
While you reached a higher plane
Studying Cobbett* and his friends,
Absorbed in the past
But chained to the future.

You are with the angels now, searching
Among the spirits for those far-off ancestors
Who will provide answers to all your questions.

Lend me your pen and guide my hand to
Fashion words that span the generations.

In the stillness of the evening I hear
The tip-tap of your white stick
And wait expectantly for your welcoming voice.

* An ancestor of Jane

To Lisl

The branches tap and knock against the pane.
Blossom scents the air through the open window.
You gave me the tree long ago, a cutting from your own,
A few small leaves, roots stretching and searching
The damp soil below.

You smiled that day, so fair, so fair
With light streaming through your shining hair.
'Look, watch, water', you said, 'and daily
I will talk to you, whisper my love from the clouds,
Send words floating through the firmament,
Witnessing your promise to remember.'

You departed years ago. With my tears I watered
Your tree. Still it grows, murmurs with branches
Touching the glass. Love comes again.

Always I keep my promise.

I look, feel, stroke its bark and
Each day remember.

Dulwich, where the Dill Grows.

Of what shall I tell you my friends?
Of past gems of production
Set in the goodness of time?
Of whispered clutches and touches on stages?
Of romances and glances in youth?

In truth, time passes, memories fade,
Loves are laid to rest. Yet the zest for life
Is reborn each morn as the sun rises.
I smile to hear you all say,

"To Bobby, our friend, a
Happy 92nd Birthday."

Footsteps to 90

Bobby Remembers

I had not thought to dance through so much time.
Small steps in childhood, faltering, exploratory.
Bounding into youth with leaps confident,
Transporting characters in stages, on stages.

I have lived my life through ballet, music, tempo,
The echoes of shoes on wood, gestures and
Touches of greater passion, evoking the
Admiration of friends and strangers.

My steps are slower now, but with eyes still bright,
Intellect untouched, smile and humour intact,
I pick up my pen to write, to celebrate
A milestone in life, the joy of recollection.

The Right To Choose

The Roman soldier fell upon his sword.
Brave Hannibal engulfed his house in flames.
A Chinese youth, protesting to the last,
Risked flattening by an advancing tank.
The fanatic blew himself to pieces in the wind
Surrounded by the nameless ones who had no wish to die.

Yet you lie there upon your hospital bed
Unseeing, unheeding, fed and watered lovingly
But never granted here the right to die,
Imprisoned in a shell from which there's no escape.

Why slumbers now that brain which wakened others,
Inspired a generation of eager scientific minds ?
That smile encouraging students to explore
Their own and others' limitations,
Cross continents, discover, advance our knowledge.

If I could free you from your enclosed world
To hold a moment's conversation, find out
Where and how you want to go,
What would you choose? What could I then fulfil?

I kiss your cheek for my remembrances,
For my indulgences, my inner peace.
Only I pray that Death will take you soon,
And all your suffering and mine will cease.

Rememberings

In the lime gold sweep of
The tree against the window,
Its branches pointing, beckoning,
Tapping out a message,
I draw closer to you.

Wander down the garden once more
In sunlight or in evening shade,
Feeling your presence, catching a
Glimpse of something in the trees.

Only a solitary thrush on the lawn
Makes movement now, cocks its head,
Then flies heavenwards out of sight,
To sing from above.

You are so close, yet not so close
That I can touch you.
Your song has ended but
The melody lingers still.

Immortality

You send me consolation
From the land of the Afterwards.
Through your life, thoughts and actions
You created your own immortality.

Ours will lie in others' remembrances;
The passing gesture we gave, the smile, the frown,
The gentle admonition, all lingering
In the mind of someone, somewhere,
To spring to life again unbidden,
Or coaxed from years past
By a laugh recalled, a sound, a scent.

We treasure each fleeting moment
Gone in an eyelid's flicker.

Afterwards

You will find me among the flowers –
No, not the florists' ones, stiff unscented,
Controlled – but among the abandoned ones,
Seeded by the winds, blessed by heavenly rain,
Coloured by Nature's unrivalled palette.

The white hollyhock by the front door,
Pushing up the patio stones with hidden strength,
Spoiling men's mosaics with greater passion.
Bronze fennel by the middle window.
Weeds misnamed, that spill their purple
Down the paths to glow like Wordsworth's violet.

Touch the lilac. Breathe the scented daphne.
Admire the shadings of the viburnum.

I will linger there to help you, heal your troubles,
Grow in your thoughts, watered by your tears.

www.ingramcontent.com/pod-product-compliance
Ingram Content Group UK Ltd.
Pitfield, Milton Keynes, MK11 3LW, UK
UKHW041642190726
13854UKWH00006B/2656